"NOBODY LIKES ME"

"Nobody likes me"

HELPING YOUR CHILD MAKE FRIENDS

Elaine K. McEwan

Harold Shaw Publishers
Wheaton, Illinois

Cover design by David LaPlaca
Edited by Esther Waldrop

ISBN 0-87788-590-7

Library of Congress Cataloging-in-Publication Data

McEwan, Elaine K., 1941-
   "Nobody likes me" : helping your child make friends / by Elaine
  K. McEwan.
     p.   cm.
   ISBN 0-87788-590-7
   1. Friendship—Study and teaching. 2. Friendship in children.
   3. Social skills—Study and teaching. 4. Social skills in children.
   5. Child rearing. I. Title.
   HQ784.F7M34   1996
   649'.1—dc20   96-3840
                                         CIP

02 01 00 99 98 97

10 9 8 7 6 5 4 3 2

Contents

1
Why Don't Kids Like Other Kids?

Ian was a bright sixth grader. He got straight *As*, so his parents weren't worried about under-achievement. But they were in my office several times each month with concerns about his social problems. Ian didn't have any friends. He was constantly picked on during recess and was never chosen for a team in gym class. His parents were almost willing to buy him some friends if I could have recommended a store where they could be purchased.

Susan's mother waited until ten o'clock one night to call me at home. "Are you aware," she challenged me in an indignant voice, "of the problem that exists in the sixth grade?" I imagined sex and drugs, judging from the time of night and her attitude. "There are," she announced, "cliques among the sixth-grade girls." I immediately knew the reason for her call—her daughter wasn't in a clique. The distraught girl had been crying on her mother's shoulder for the past half hour.

As an elementary-school principal, I confronted almost daily the anguish and frustration that faced parents when their children didn't fit in. We hurt for our kids when they don't have friends. And the worst part about it is we often feel powerless to do anything. Your child comes home from school and complains about getting teased on the bus or not ever getting picked to be on a kickball team until your heart begins to break. When quizzed about why, she usually doesn't have a clue. You get angry and resentful and march off to school, ready to do battle with the powers that be.

You can't hire a tutor to teach your child social skills. Teachers aren't usually that concerned about minor squabbles between elementary-school kids. They address issues as they occur on the playground but often don't see their primary role as one of social arbiter. They see a child who is constantly coming to them with complaints as a whiner or a sissy. What's a parent to do? Don't panic. There are some steps you can take to solve this problem. But you'll have to begin by looking at your child through the eyes of his or her peers. That's not an easy thing to do. Most of us don't really want to hear the bad news, yet sometimes that's precisely what is needed if we really want to solve the problem. Take off your rose-colored glasses and be realistic.

Jason, an intense first-grader, was sitting at the round table in my office with his parents. Jason was already a social outcast at the tender age of six, and I could tell that his parents were defensive and full of blame. Surely if I were a better principal and his teacher were more effective, Jason would have loads of friends and be having a great year in first grade. Jason had received a detention from the art teacher for hitting one of his classmates. His parents were protesting the unfairness of Jason's consequence. He assured his parents that he had done no such thing. They were mystified as to why we were picking on Jason. Obviously, we had a serious communication breakdown here. I needed the wisdom of Solomon and the eloquence of Churchill to come out of this conference alive. Suddenly I had an inspiration. I would ask Jason to reenact the scene for me. Perhaps the truth would come out. Jason was eager to participate.

"I didn't do anything," he assured me. "She wouldn't leave me alone."

"What did she do?" I asked. His parents were silent observers. "Well," he said slowly, "she put her elbow in my space."

"Like this?" I demonstrated, sliding my elbow into his "space."

"Yeah," he agreed with a big smile.

"So, what did you do then?" I asked.

"Oh, nothing," he said.

"Show me," I suggested.

Jason cocked his elbow and slammed it into the side of my body. He was not subtle.

Both of his parents were wide-eyed.

"Well," I said, "I think that solves the problem of what happened. Would you both agree that Jason will be staying after school?"

They weren't sure what to say. I felt like Perry Mason! The criminal had confessed. But my glee was short lived, because I knew that this was only one of many conferences I would have with Jason and his

parents over the years to come. Neither Jason nor his
parents were ready to come to grips with the serious
social problems that were going to plague him through-
out his school years unless they were soberly and se-
riously dealt with immediately.

Why Doesn't Your Child Have Friends?

Friendship for children is multidimensional and complex. Adults (parents and teachers) who would dismiss
the social interactions that take place on the playground and in the classroom as "childish" fail to re-
alize that the seeds of self-esteem, social awareness,
and future success are being sown here. Childhood
and adolescent friendship has many facets, and helping your child to make friends successfully is an important undertaking.

The reasons behind *your* child's lack of acceptance
may not be like Jason's, but they will generally be
related to one or more of the following: the characteristics of the school and community, the characteristics of your child, and/or the behavior of your
child.

**1. Characteristics and culture of the school and
neighborhood.** It is from the school and the neighborhood that your children choose many (although not
all) of their friends. If the prevailing dress code calls
for black T-shirts and shaved heads and your child
wears chinos and button-downs, he probably won't be
the most popular kid on the block. If the majority of
your child's peer group does not value good behavior
or good grades, then it's not likely he will win points

among his peers for being smart and well behaved. If the majority of students in your child's school do not share the same work ethic, values, or moral standards as your family, then your child will have a difficult time developing positive social relationships.

Parents who do not have the option of home-schooling their child or sending her to a private school need to help her process these conflicts. Explaining your family's values to your child, offering support when her peers challenge those values, and praising her when she chooses to uphold them will foster her self-reliance and confidence in what is right.

I had this kind of experience when I was in elementary school. In my three-room country school I was an oddity. I wore new clothes, I read books, and I was a Christian. I didn't have many friends in that environment, but I survived. When I went to high school in the city, I made lots of new friends. I discovered it wasn't me; it was the culture of my school that created my social problems. Surviving in this kind of environment takes tough skin and lots of support from home. My mother always told me it was a character-building experience. She had more faith than I did at the time, but she was right. Solving social problems in a hostile environment takes finesse.

2. Characteristics of your child. Who your child is will also make a difference.

If your child is very sensitive, mature, or gifted, he can often experience traumatic social difficulties. He may be resented by classmates for the ease with which he handles academic tasks; he may feel more comfortable relating to adults than to his peers; and he may place a higher value on intellectual pursuits than on extracurricular activities.

If your child has a disability, together you will face a different kind of challenge. An encouraging educational program now being implemented in schools is inclusive education. This program includes students with severe disabilities in the regular education program. But many schools around the country still separate children with disabilities from their peers. Work with the educators in your community to bring about change. Students with learning disabilities or ADHD (Attention Deficit Hyperativity Disorder) will often find it difficult to pick up on social cues and may behave in ways that are not age-appropriate or socially acceptable. Finding ways to overcome these social deficits is just as important as solving your child's academic problems.

Your child's appearance will definitely affect her social development. Although you need not give in to every clothing fad that looms on the horizon, most children like to wear what everyone else is wearing. Ian's parents were oblivious to the social impact of making him wear corduroys when everyone else was wearing blue jeans.

If it is within your financial means, utilize the services of orthodontists, opthalmologists, orthopedic surgeons, and dermatologists to make sure your children have straight teeth, attractive glasses or contact lenses, straight legs, and clear skin. Problems of this nature can severely influence children's self-confidence and expose them to unnecessary teasing.

At the same time, find ways to assure them that their inner character is more important than their outer appearance. Although we can't change who our children are, we can help them celebrate their strengths and compensate for their weaknesses.

Your child's temperament and personality may predispose him to be shy and withdrawn. He may find it difficult to reach out and make the first move. His reticence may make it difficult for him to make friends, but shyness can usually be overcome through maturity, some social skills training, and encouragement from parents.

Although the maturity level of your child, the environment, your child's appearance, or her shy nature can have an impact on her social acceptance and ability to make friends, it's a rare child who can't overcome these problems with parental support and encouragement. Your child will eventually find her niche. The final source of social problems is, I'm afraid, a horse of a different color.

3. Behavior of your child. A child's behavior can often be the primary source of social problems. As an elementary school principal, I faced several types of children with what I choose to call "behavioral" social problems: the child who threatens and intimidates other children, the class bully; the child who acts the part of court jester and seeks the attention of others; the child who looks for recognition and acceptance from adults because he is unable to relate to his peers;

the child who is totally self-centered, rude, boorish, sometimes cruel, or totally socially unaware (for any number of reasons, which we'll talk about later); the child who attempts to buy friendship with gifts and bribes; and the child who just can't seem to do anything right when it comes to making and keeping friends—he is a walking encyclopedia of "friendship faux pas."

Here are just a few of the more common mistakes that keep children from having smooth sailing on the seas of friendship.

- Sharing personal secrets too readily
- Telling secrets that others have shared in confidence
- Being bossy; telling people what to do rather than asking
- Bragging or thinking he/she is better than everyone else
- Being a know-it-all
- Getting into many fights
- Always wanting to be first
- Making fun of others
- Always thinking that people are picking on him/her
- Making sounds that bother other people (burping, sniffing)
- Lying to get what he/she wants
- Being critical of others
- Constantly interrupting when others are talking
- Becoming angry easily, especially when others win

- Not knowing when to leave
- Being too direct and blunt
- Trying to have friendships that exclude others
- Rushing a friendship and scaring off the other person
- Saying the wrong things
- Doing things that disgust others (e.g., picking one's nose or making strange noises while eating)
- Trying to break into a group that's not right for him/her
- Talking too much
- Not being willing to share
- Not being willing to compromise (always needing to have his/her way)
- Not being willing to forgive and forget if a friend makes a mistake
- Gossiping about friends to others

All of these behaviors create serious problems for the children who exhibit them. Nobody likes them. Even the adults in their lives—teachers, principals, Sunday school teachers, and coaches—have a hard time maintaining a positive attitude. If your child doesn't have any friends, you need to take some proactive steps immediately.

What Causes These Social Problems?

Sometimes the reason children have social problems is because they simply do not know how to respond appropriately. For that child, simple instruction is enough. Other children may have the knowledge but haven't had sufficient opportunity to practice the social skills. When social problems are severe, however, the cause is more complex. Emotions such as anxiety, fear, and anger may be standing in the way of appropriate social responses. Children may have been living with unsuitable role models and have learned bad habits. Or perhaps they have been reinforced for inappropriate behaviors over a long period of time, and since they've worked so well with Mom and Dad, they're now "taking their show on the road."

For each child I've encountered in the school setting who has severe behavioral social problems, I can usually identify some things his parents are doing to help the cause along. Too many of us are surprisingly oblivious to the power of our spoken word and the daily example we set. We're programming our kids to be social dropouts.

We'd all like to think that we do a better job than the parents I'm going to describe in a minute. The problem is, we're only human! I'm a parent too. I blush with embarassment when I think of my behavior when I went in to see the principal about a social problem my son was having in middle school. I was a textbook case of the overprotective, pitying parent. It couldn't have been more obvious unless I'd worn a flashing neon sign. I also cringe with shame when I recall the mini-tantrum I threw when confronting my daughter's elementary school principal. My competitive and materialistic spirit was on display for all to see, including my daughter. Where our children are concerned, we can, and frequently do, lose all objectivity. I beg of you, if your child is having social problems, think about changing your own behavior as you work on helping your child to make friends more readily. As you read the following descriptions, try not to be defensive. If you recognize even a smidgen of your own attitudes and behavior here, clean house at home. Don't be offended!

The rejecting parents. These parents obviously feel their child must have popped up in the wrong family. "She's just impossible. We can't do a thing with her at home either. Nobody can get along with her."

The pitying parents. These parents feel so sorry for their child. They agonize over the terrible plight she is in and wring their hands in despair. "I don't know what's to become of her. She just doesn't seem to be able to get along with anybody."

The authoritarian parents. When Mr. and Mrs. Authoritarian arrive in my office, they expect silence and subservience from everyone. "We're going to get to the bottom of this problem if it's the last thing we do. Now, obviously you don't run a very tight ship around here. If you had better discipline on your playground, my son wouldn't have to worry about getting pushed around."

The inconsistent parents. This wishy-washy pair can't decide how to handle any situation. "Okay, you can do it this time, but never again. Well, whatever you think we ought to do." They send a clear message that whatever they say is open for negotiation. They haven't had an original thought about their children in years and are running scared.

The suspicious parents. These folks are looking for a plot (could be the secular humanists; could be the school board; could be the teachers; could be the books in the library). Somebody, somewhere, has it in for their kid, and they're going to find out the reason why. It certainly isn't the kid's fault. That's for certain.

The hostile and angry parents. These parents are mad at the world, and somebody forgot to tell them that their anger is rubbing off on their children. They isolate themselves from adult friendships and take their children along for the ride.

The valueless parents. Parents without values are hard to deal with. They don't subscribe to the usual discussion about "right and wrong." For them it's all relative. Whatever works, do it. "Nobody's going to push our kid around. Look out for Number One. That's our rule."

The disparaging parents. This parent goes beyond subtle rejection to outright vilification. "You never were too bright." "We should have shipped you off to military school when you were born." "Are you dumb, or what?"

The materialistic parent. These parents don't have time to come to school for a meeting. Telephone calls go unanswered. You only reach a secretary or voice mail. The job is more important than the child. Things are more important than kids. These parents have little time or energy to give to their family. They are too busy making money and often leave parenting to paid lackeys.

The overprotective parent. These parents are constantly rescuing their child from the discipline of other people. When the Little League coach calls with a problem, it's his fault. When the teacher shares a concern, she doesn't understand. When a neighbor reports an incident, he's a troublemaker, rather than your child. The overprotective parent never lets his child face the music without intervening. Overprotective parents are always rewriting the way it really happened.

The abusive and neglectful parent. This parent engenders fear and hostility in the eyes of the child: a flinch of the shoulder when a hand is raised; an aggressive and abusive vocabulary laden with obscenities. "Just wait until we get home. I'll show you who's boss."

Nothing is good enough for this parent. "You've really let me down this time" is the hallmark of the parent with impossibly high standards. Highly successful parents with an unsuccessful child, they have no sympathy or empathy, only standards. They never offer strategies or support, only blame.

The competitive parent. "You've got to get first place or I won't love you" is the mantra of the competitive parent. The child tries overly hard to please and becomes obnoxious in the process.

Sorry for the guilt trip we just took. I often take brief ones myself. Guilt is not bad if it forces us to change from unproductive to productive behaviors. I know it's hard to see ourselves as others see us. If your child doesn't have any friends and frequently whines, "Nobody likes me," there are dozens of things you can do to help, many of them painless and very entertaining. The following chapters will be filled with great ideas. But they'll all be worthless if you think only in terms of changing your child. Be willing to change yourself in the process.

2

What Can We Do at Home?

Somehow in my naiveté as a fledgling teacher, I believed that children came to school to learn. "Oh, no," my fifth-grade class corrected me one day when we were talking about the purpose of school, "we come to school to be with our friends." But what if your child doesn't have any friends? What's the outlook for having a good day at school (or anywhere) then?

Although the social expertise that enables us to make and keep friends begins to develop as early as infancy, most parents usually aren't aware of "friendship problems" until the middle elementary grades. Children in kindergarten through second grade develop friendships based more on proximity than on any sense of loyalty or affection. But suddenly the concept of "popularity" rears its ugly head and alignments and cliques begin to form. By middle school, friendships are much more intense and are definitely based on variables such as personality, ability levels, common interests, and shared values. When your child is on the outside looking in, life is miserable for all concerned.

Assessing Your Child's Friendship Quotient

If your child is complaining about a lack of friends and social problems, or if you notice that your child is exhibiting the early warning signs of social problems, now is the time to do some research. Does she have a hard time getting along with other children in the neighborhood? Is she moody, bad-tempered, or unpleasant toward her siblings? Does she spend a lot of time in her room, uncommunicative and sullen?

Your child's teacher can often be a source of information. Make an appointment for a conference, and ask the teacher the following questions to help you determine the severity of the problem:

- Does my child participate in group activities and class discussions, or is he a loner in the class?
- Is my child included in play activities at recess (elementary school) or extracurricular activities (middle school or high school), or is she turning her classmates off?
- Does my child engage in any specific behaviors that other children find unattractive? What are they?
- Does he work independently, or is he asking for help and reassurance constantly?

- Does she have any friends at all in the class? Who are they, and how did the friendship get started?
- What strategies have you, as the teacher, used to try to help my child?
- Do you find my child unattractive? Are you tempted to put him down in class? (You'll have to be subtle in asking this question, but it can be done. The teacher has a professional responsibility to nurture and develop your child's self-esteem.)

When your child was small, it was easy to invite a few neighborhood children over to play and eavesdrop on what was going on. As your child gets older, you will only have her word about what is really happening. That's why it's important to find a relatively objective third party (like a teacher or coach) to give you the real story. This is not an easy thing to do. Telling a parent that a child has problems takes courage, tact, and kindness. Not everyone is able to do it. Hopefully you can find someone to trust.

Depending on the age of your child, you might also wish to administer the following Student Skill Checklist (appropriate for middle elementary through high-school age). Younger students may need to have the questions read aloud to them and possibly explained. Answers that receive a rating of 3, 4, or 5 should give parents little or no concern. And most children will have a sprinkling of 1s and 2s as well. But if a child has a majority of 1s and 2s, parents should consider seeking professional assistance. Although the checklist is a bit intimidating in size, the results will give you valuable information about where to start coaching your child in social skills.

Student Social Skill Checklist[1]

Directions:

Each of the questions will ask you about how well you do something. Next to each question is a number.

Circle number 1	If you almost never do what the question asks.
Circle number 2	If you seldom do it.
Circle number 3	If you sometimes do it.
Circle number 4	If you do it often.
Circle number 5	If you almost always do it.

There are no right or wrong answers to these questions. Answer the way you really feel about each question.

Ratings:	Almost Never	Seldom	Sometimes	Often	Almost Always
	1	2	3	4	5

1. Is it easy for me to listen to someone who is talking to me?

    1   2   3   4   5

2. Do I ask for help in a friendly way when I need the help?

    1   2   3   4   5

3. Do I tell people thank you for something they have done for me?

    1   2   3   4   5

4. Do I have the materials I need for my classes (like books, pencils, paper)?

     1   2   3   4   5

5. Do I understand what to do when directions are given, and do I follow these directions?

     1   2   3   4   5

6. Do I finish my schoolwork?

     1   2   3   4   5

7. Do I join in on class talks or discussions?

     1   2   3   4   5

8. Do I try to help an adult when I think he/she could use the help?

     1   2   3   4   5

9. Do I decide what I don't understand about my schoolwork and ask my teacher the question in a friendly way?

     1   2   3   4   5

10. Is it easy for me to keep doing my schoolwork when people are noisy?

     1   2   3   4   5

11. Do I fix mistakes on my work without getting upset?

     1   2   3   4   5

12. Do I choose something to do when I have free time?

     1   2   3   4   5

13. Do I decide on something I want to work for and keep working until I get it?

     1   2   3   4   5

14. Is it easy for me to take the first step to meet somebody I don't know?

     1   2   3   4   5

15. Is it easy for me to start a conversation with someone?

     1   2   3   4   5

16. When I have something else I have to do, do I end a conversation with someone in a nice way?

     1   2   3   4   5

17. Do I ask to join in a game or activity in a friendly way?

     1   2   3   4   5

18. Do I follow the rules when I play a game?

     1   2   3   4   5

19. Is it easy for me to ask a favor of someone?

     1   2   3   4   5

20. Do I notice when somebody needs help and try to help them?

     1   2   3   4   5

21. Do I tell others that I like something nice about them or something nice they have done for me or for somebody else?

     1   2   3   4   5

22. When someone says they like something about me, do I accept what they say?

     1   2   3   4   5

23. Do I suggest things to do with my friends?

     1   2   3   4   5

24. Am I willing to share my things with others?

     1   2   3   4   5

25. Do I tell others I'm sorry after I do something wrong?

     1   2   3   4   5

26. Do I know how I feel about different things that happen?

     1   2   3   4   5

27. Do I let others know what I am feeling and do it in a good way?

    1   2   3   4   5

28. Do I try to determine how other people are feeling?

    1   2   3   4   5

29. Do I show others that I understand how they feel?

    1   2   3   4   5

30. When someone has a problem, do I let them know that I understand how they feel?

    1   2   3   4   5

31. When I am angry, do I deal with it in ways that won't hurt other people?

    1   2   3   4   5

32. Do I try to understand other people's angry feelings?

    1   2   3   4   5

33. Do I let others know I care about them?

    1   2   3   4   5

34. Do I know what makes me afraid and do I think of things to do so I don't stay afraid?

    1   2   3   4   5

35. Do I say and do nice things for myself when I have earned it?

    1   2   3   4   5

36. Do I control my temper when I am upset?

    1   2   3   4   5

37. Do I know when I have to ask to do something I want to do, and do I ask in a friendly way?

    1   2   3   4   5

38. When somebody teases me, do I stay in control?

    1   2   3   4   5

39. Do I try to stay away from things that may get me into trouble?

    1   2   3   4   5

40. Do I think of ways other than fighting to take care of problems?

    1   2   3   4   5

41. Do I think of ways to deal with a problem and think of what might happen if I use these ways?

    1   2   3   4   5

42. When I do something I shouldn't have done, do I accept what happens then?

    1   2   3   4   5

43. Do I find out what I have been accused of and why, and then think of a good way to handle it?

    1   2   3   4   5

44. When I don't agree with somebody, do I help think of a plan to make both of us happy?

    1   2   3   4   5

45. When I feel bored, do I think of good things to do and then do them?

    1   2   3   4   5

46. Can I tell when a problem happened because of something I did?

    1   2   3   4   5

47. Do I tell others without getting mad or yelling when they have caused a problem for me?

    1   2   3   4   5

48. Do I help think of a fair way to take care of a complaint against me?

    1   2   3   4   5

49. When I lose at a game, do I keep from getting upset?

    1   2   3   4   5

50. Do I tell others something good about the way they played a game?

        1   2   3   4   5

51. Do I decide if I have been left out, and then do things in a good way to make me feel better?

        1   2   3   4   5

52. Do I do things that will help me feel less embarrassed?

        1   2   3   4   5

53. When I don't do well with something (on a test, doing my chores), do I decide ways I could do better next time?

        1   2   3   4   5

54. When I am told no, can I keep from becoming upset?

        1   2   3   4   5

55. Do I say no to things that might get me into trouble or that I don't want to do, and do I say it in a friendly way?

        1   2   3   4   5

56. Can I keep my body from getting tight and tense when I'm angry or upset?

        1   2   3   4   5

57. When a group of kids wants me to do something that might get me in trouble or that is wrong, do I say no?

        1   2   3   4   5

58. Do I keep from taking things that aren't mine?

        1   2   3   4   5

59. Is it easy for me to decide what to do when I'm given a choice?

        1   2   3   4   5

60. Do I tell the truth about what I have done, even
    if I might get into trouble?
               1   2   3   4   5

What Is Your Family's Friendship Quotient?

After you have considered your child's ability to relate
socially to other children as well as adults, assess your
family's ability to relate in a positive way to one another.

Does your child know that you like him? Do you
give him praise and positive feedback when appropriate? When children feel secure and self-confident at
home, they will be willing to take risks (even in the
face of possible rejection) in a wider social arena.
Model love and acceptance in your home.

Is your home a friendly place? Do you give your
child a chance to experience social success at home?
This is especially important for very young children.
Don't let your child be teased, bullied, or embarrassed
when she is very young. This can traumatize your
child into the avoidance of others as she matures. Depending on the age of your child, have activities going
on that your child and his peers enjoy, such as bike-
riding, board games, or sports.

**Does your family engage in cooperative activi-
ties** that give everyone a chance to practice social
skills? Go out for a bite to eat together, play Trivial
Pursuit, rake leaves, or go bowling. Every family should

have its list of enjoyable things to do together. These family activities will give you a chance to see how well your child is learning how to get along.

Are you sensitive to the social skills that are appropriate and necessary for each age group? Preschoolers need to learn the basic rules of relating to others such as taking turns, sharing, complimenting others, and contributing ideas for games. Older children need to know how to give and take and talk with peers about common interests.

Do you minimize criticism and negativity (about other family members, family "friends," neighbors, and especially any friends that your child may have)? Of course it's important to have standards and values, but if *no one* is ever "good enough" to measure up to *your* family's standards, you'll run the risk of your child feeling he'll never be able to please you in the choice of his friends. He'll either totally shut you out of any friendship choices or become a complete social recluse.

Do you talk about, read about, and model character traits that are desirable in friends? Friends are generous, sharing, considerate, and cooperative. They have a good sense of humor and are cheerful. They are good sports whether they win or lose. Do you point out character traits that make children (and adults) unpopular and friendless? Children who tease, who gloat when they win and cry when they lose, or who are bossy, insulting, or tattletales certainly aren't at the top of any popularity poll.

Do you give your child breathing room to make some decisions on her own? Don't take *total* responsibility for organizing your child's social life. Even toddlers can make some simple social decisions on their own.

How can you solve the problem that is confronting your family?

Let's summarize the steps you can take to help your child make and keep friends.

Develop an accurate assessment and profile of your child's problem. Complete the questionnaire given on pages 24–30. Consult with other significant adults who interact with your child, and talk with your child to get his perspective.

Examine your family environment. Are there problems in your home that could be contributing to your child's social problems? Does your child's behavior mirror that of another family member? Can you identify any of the unhealthy home environments that we described earlier as being present in your home?

Seek professional help. Depending on the severity of the problem, consult a pastoral counselor, psychologist, or social worker. Ask school administrators if they have access to (or can refer you to) professionals who specialize in helping parents and teachers with children's behavior.

There are times when we are too close to a problem to be objective. Our deep love and concern for our children stands in the way of facing some difficult truths, especially if *we* are part of the problem. That's when to get help from others.

Work cooperatively with school professionals. Solving your child's problem requires everyone's cooperation. Listen carefully to what the teacher and principal say about your child's behavior. If you are defensive, argumentative, or hostile, you might waste valuable time that could be used to help your child.

Begin to build social skill development into the fabric of your home. The following suggestions are valuable for children of all ages. Look for references to future chapters, where more in-depth information will be shared.

Show your child how to be a friend to others. Chapter 3 will describe how you can teach your child to be friendly, and chapter 4 will provide social skill-building lessons to use with your child. You will also find additional books listed in the Resource section at the end of the book.

Spend one-on-one time with your child on a regular basis. As an elementary-school principal, I frequently worked with children who had encountered serious social difficulties. They had no one to spend time with them. I would often take one or more to McDonald's for lunch, where we would practice the fine art of social conversation. It was obvious in many cases that this was the first time anyone had

ever given this child thirty minutes of uninter-
rupted attention. All children need this kind of attention from their parents.

The activities in which you engage should be of
the child's own choosing. They could involve playing a game, making cupcakes, or just lying on the
bed to talk. Make sure that nothing interrupts this
together-time.

Model good social skills. Give your child a chance
to see you in appropriate social interaction. Invite
teachers to your home for lunch or dinner. Invite
your child to join you if you go places with adult
friends. One word of warning, however. Some children are perfectly comfortable with adults and in
fact prefer them. If your child falls into that cate-
gory, you will need to focus your attention on helping her to build healthy peer relationships.

Use praise whenever you can. I know that when
your child is complaining endlessly about the fact
that nobody likes him, you find it difficult to be
positive and upbeat. But try it! You'll like it!

Plan cooperative family activities. Organize some
activities that give your family a chance to practice
social skills. These activities will give you a chance
to see how well your child is learning some of the
lessons you have been teaching her. Chapter 5 contains "fifty fabulous cooperative activities to build
family friendships."

Read aloud. Use good stories to teach the values
of friendship and loyalty. There is much outstanding children's fiction that demonstrates through the
printed word what a real friendship is all about.

Plan ahead. When my children were young, we would often practice how to behave if we were going to be heading into a new social situation. I'd play the parts and demonstrate what my children should say and do to be socially acceptable. If your child has an explosive temper or tends to say the wrong thing, role-play situations of this type to give him the opportunity to practice appropriate responses.

Talk through your day. Debrief at the end of each day, not in the spirit of criticism, but in the spirit of teamwork and "How can I do better tomorrow?" The more you talk about what your child should be doing and let her know that you expect her behavior to change, the greater the chance that a change will actually occur.

Make your home a friendly place. You might consider inviting some of your children's peers into your home to participate in some of the activities in chapter 5, and observe the children's interaction, both positive and negative.

Help your child's teacher build social skills in the classroom. If you can, suggest to your child's teachers that they use some cooperative learning activities in the classroom. Cooperative classrooms (rather than competitive ones) foster academic achievement as well as positive social adjustment.

Peer pairing and buddy system. If a teacher expects that students will work together and help each other, there is a greater likelihood that this will happen. If a teacher fosters individualization and doesn't let students interact at all during the school day, children are at a disadvantage when it comes to developing their social skills.

Debriefing sessions. The skilled classroom teacher allows time after a cooperative activity to talk about what happened and why it did or didn't work. Children learn to label their behaviors, and to praise and reward those students who exhibit positive behaviors.

Special plans for special cases. If your child is suffering from a truly severe social problem, ask for a consultation with the school psychologist or behavioral counselor. They are skilled in working with classroom teachers and students to enlist their help for your child. They often use programs that have been designed to teach social skills in a classroom setting.

Jackie, a fourth grader, was bossy, mean, rude, and outspoken. Nobody wanted to be in the same room with her, let alone work cooperatively with her. She had other troubles at home—abusive older brothers and a reputation as a scapegoat—that complicated her social life at school.

Jackie's problems had been present for some time, but by the fourth grade, when children become more socially selective, her peers weren't willing to overlook them anymore. We enlisted the help of the school psychologist and behavioral counselor, who gave Jackie special training in social skills. They also gave her classmates ideas about how to reinforce and praise the positive things that she was learning to do. With the cooperation of her classmates and parents, Jackie began to learn to make and keep friends.

Utilize the church and community to help your child fit in.

Special programs. Scouts, park district programs, YMCAs, and other groups can provide recreational programs along with opportunities to meet peers.

Church groups. Youth groups at church are the perfect place to use newly developing social skills. Awana and Pioneer Clubs are wonderful activities. Friendship, loyalty, and kindness should be found in abundance in these settings, especially from the adults involved in sponsorship.

Build on the strengths and enhance the skills of your child.

Social games and skills. Make sure your child knows how to bowl, play volleyball, or roller skate if those activities could help him to develop socially. There's nothing worse than being a wallflower at a social gathering because you don't have the skills to participate.

Special interests. Figure out what your child's real strengths are. Give her lessons. Karate lessons are often a real ego boost for children who are having social problems. The discipline and mentoring relationships that are found as more proficient students teach novices could be very beneficial to your child. Music and art lessons often serve the same purpose.

Endnotes

1. Student Social Skill Checklist on pages 24–30 is reprinted by permission of the publisher from *Skillstreaming the Elementary School Child* by Ellen McGinnis & Arnold P. Goldstein (Champaign, Ill.: Research Press Company, 1984).

3

Can I Teach My Child to Be Friendly?

Knowing how to make and keep friends seems like something you should just grow up knowing how to do, like walking and talking. Or at the very most, it shouldn't be any harder than learning to tie your shoes or ride a bicycle. If that were the case, however, an entire industry of self-help books would collapse under the sheer weight of unsold volumes.

Making and keeping friends is a complex social act made up of hundreds of nuances of verbal and nonverbal communication, character and personality traits, mixed in with big doses of self-confidence and self-worth. No wonder that few of us emerge unscathed from our friendship experiences. Adults have just as many problems with friends as children do.

All of us can use a little coaching in the social skills needed to make and keep friends.

What Are the Social Skills Your Child Needs to Make and Keep Friends?

If you've looked ahead to the next chapter, you've probably panicked at the length of the list. But don't worry! You can't possibly teach all of these skills immediately, particularly if your child is shy or is lacking many of them, so don't even try! But you should begin to informally (and possibly formally) assess your child and determine which skills are needed most. You may determine that there are just a few that need polishing. Or you may have lots of work to do. But the job can be done with patience and love.

In chapter 4 we'll consider each skill individually, break it down into its component parts, and give you a mini lesson plan. Just remember that what may be an age-appropriate skill level for a four- or five-year-old will be much different from what is expected from a teenager. But the basic skills remain the same. Use common sense.

Your child will need basic conversational skills, which include things like being able to introduce one's self to new people, being able to wait one's turn in a conversation, and knowing how to end a conversation. Another set of skills focus on your child's interaction with peers. These include being able to share, compromise, and handle being teased, and knowing how to apologize. The third set of skills concern emotional control and deal with issues like handling anger, being able to lose gracefully, and knowing what to do when you're embarassed. Finally, you'll learn about two overall skills that are crucial to social maturity: being able to understand how behavior has an impact on others, and being able to understand one's own behavior.

What Are the Steps to Teaching a Social Skill?

The first step in teaching a specific social skill is understanding the individual components of the skill. In order to teach it to your child, you will have to break it down, explain what it looks like, tell your child situations in which he should or shouldn't use the skill, give him some concrete examples, and then follow the steps below.

Model the skill. Present the model in a clear and detailed manner, and demonstrate the behavior. There is no substitute for your child seeing someone else do what you want her to do. Present the steps from least difficult to most difficult behaviors. Repeat this step as often as necessary, even going overboard to make sure that each skill is understood. Don't include any irrelevant details or extraneous material that might confuse your child. It might be helpful to use several different methods of modeling the behavior, such as puppets, tapes, magazines, newspapers, movies, TV shows, stories, peers, and family members.

Practice the skill in a guided or supervised setting. Include other family members in a practice session, but make sure that everyone is supportive and

41

encouraging. No laughing, name calling, or teasing is permitted. Rehearsing is absolutely essential before you send your child out into the "real world."

Give feedback, praise, and reinforcement. Make sure that your child's efforts are appreciated. This is hard work for a child who is lagging behind in social development. He needs all the encouragement you can give. Here are some examples of encouraging words you can give your child. Try to make your compliments as specific as possible. A child who lacks self-esteem will find it much easier to accept that one person loved what he did, even if he can't accept that on a global scale his work is beyond measure.

- Excellent piece of work.
- Super. That's the way to do it.
- Your fine work pleases me.
- Good; keep plugging.
- That was very creative.
- Good thinking.
- You should be proud of your effort.
- That's a marked improvement.
- That's a better way to go about it.
- I'm proud of your work.
- Keep trying.
- That's the way to work at it.
- That's outstanding.
- Don't give up. You can do it.
- That was a good decision. It shows thought.
- Nice effort.
- Keep working. You're making progress.

Practice in a "real world" situation. Now is the time to send your child out to practice in the "real world." You'll have to have faith in her ability.

Debrief on how things are going. Talk with your child about how it went. Be a good listener, and avoid jumping in with critical remarks and comments designed to discourage.

You can see that social skill training is not a "quick fix." The process will take time and patience. It's not enough to say to your child, "Be polite," or "Be nicer to people." Those instructions are much too vague. For the child who is having a hard time making friends, you will need to suggest specific steps similar to those found in the complete list of social skills in the next chapter.

4

Social Skills Your Child Needs to Know

During the five years before we had children, my husband and I vacationed at a lovely northern Wisconsin resort each summer. Dinner was served each evening in the dining room, and we were especially impressed by one family with a preschool son. He was so polite and well mannered that I talked frequently with his parents, hoping to find out the secret of their success. When we had children, I wanted them to behave just like Andrew. I wasn't always as successful as Andrew's parents had been, but that experience certainly made me aware of the importance of teaching social skills to children as they grow. Now, in hindsight, I can reflect on just how unusual Andrew was for a four-year-old, slightly precocious and perhaps even a little out of touch with his own peers. But nevertheless, thirty years later I haven't forgotten him. Social skills don't just happen to children. They need to be taught and inculcated on

45

a daily basis. And for some children, the teaching needs to be more direct and constant than for others.

This chapter describes the social skills needed by children at every age level. You might choose to create a mini-lesson for each skill, or you might give the chapter to your child to read if he's old enough. The descriptions are written in an easy-to-understand style that is appropriate for children. But be sure you take time for discussion and role-playing. And be patient. These lessons take time.

Conversational Skills

Conversational skills are needed when you are meeting and talking to people—your friends, parents, and teachers. They take lots of practice. Don't get discouraged if they seem awkward and difficult at first.

Skill #1. Meeting new people. It can be scary to go up to someone you have never met before and introduce yourself. But you can do it one step at a time. First, decide who you want to meet. Then look for someone in the group who isn't surrounded by lots of other people. Choose someone who looks as if he or she might be new. Sometimes you might want to be friends with popular people who already have lots of friends, but you might have more success if you seek out people who look like they need a friend.

Be sure to choose the right time to introduce yourself, though. Don't interrupt another conversation that is going on. Try waiting until a new activity is just beginning. Then walk up to the person and look right at him or her. Don't get too close, though. People sometimes get upset about that. Don't look down at the floor or off in another direction either. Look the person right in the eye. Then tell the person who you are. "Hi, I'm Jack," or "Hi, my name is Susan." Wait for the person to tell you his name, but if he doesn't tell you, just ask.

Tell the person something about yourself. "I'm new this year. How long have you gone to Lincoln School?" Or, if you're on the playground, tell the person what you would like to do or invite them to share an activity with you. Say, "Wanna play catch?" or "Can I join the game?" Practice with your parents, and you'll be more comfortable doing this.

Skill #2. Introducing two people who don't know each other. When you're in the middle of a conversation and someone new comes along, be ready to introduce the new person to the person with whom you're talking.

You could ask a question like "Do you two know each other?" If the answer is no, then you could say something like this: "Joan, I'd like you to meet Sally. She lives down the street from me. Sally, this is Joan." Always introduce your parents to your friends and teachers they have not met. If you are introducing someone to your parents, mention your mom or dad first. "Mom, this is my new friend Ben. Ben, this is my mom."

Skill #3. Starting a conversation. Now that you've met someone new, the next step is starting a conversation. Begin speaking in a friendly way while looking directly at the person with whom you're talking.

Talking to another person takes a lot of practice. Don't talk about sad or unpleasant things. Don't complain, whine, or criticize. Nobody wants to spend time talking to somebody who isn't any fun. Don't brag about yourself either.

If you can't think of anything to say, ask questions to find out about the other person's interests. Listen carefully to what the other person is saying so that when you answer you'll be talking about the same subject. Make sure you look right at the other person while she is talking. If you look away when someone is speaking to you, that person might think you are being rude or disrespectful.

Be ready to talk about something that interests you if the other person doesn't talk right away.

Skill #4. Listening to a conversation. The movements of your body and the expressions on your face that happen when you're listening to someone else talk are called nonverbal communication. And the things you do with your face and body are just as important as what you say. Remember these important rules (especially when you're talking with your parents or teachers):

- Face the person who is speaking, and look right into their eyes.
- Do not speak when others are speaking.
- Think about what is being said.

- Sit or stand still. Don't fidget or wiggle around.
- While you are thinking about what is being said, you can nod your head to let the person who is speaking know that you understand.
- You can also ask questions from time to time.

Skill #5. Keeping a conversation going. When two or more people are talking, everyone has a responsibility to contribute. Think of something you might say in response to what the other person is saying. Even if you don't have any new ideas to contribute, you can always say, "I agree with what you're saying."

Make sure you stay on the subject, though. People will think you're strange if you start talking about your trip to the zoo when everyone else is talking about yesterday's football game.

Skill #6. Waiting your turn to say something in a conversation. One of the hardest things to do is to find a way to get into the conversation or discussion if many people are talking at once. The trick is remembering what you have to say while waiting for a chance to say it.

Try not to be rude or interruptive. Listen carefully for clues that the person who is talking is almost finished. Show others that you are ready to talk by leaning forward, raising your hand slightly if the group is large, or making eye contact with the person who is speaking.

If someone else jumps into the conversation ahead of you, relax and pay attention to what is being said. Your turn will come.

Skill #7. Ending a conversation. Conversations can't go on forever. Knowing how to politely end a conversation without being rude is very important. It takes a lot of practice, especially if you are talking to someone who never seems to stop.

There are many reasons to end a conversation. You may have someplace to go. You may need to talk to someone else, or maybe someone is waiting to talk to you. Decide what to say so you won't get the other person upset.

This can be tricky, and you won't always be successful. Sometimes people just walk away from a conversation, not realizing that they should have worked just as hard at ending the conversation as they did at starting it.

Make sure you wait until the other person stops talking before you announce that you've enjoyed talking to them, but you need to "get to class," "talk to John," or "get to basketball practice." Make sure you end the conversation in a friendly way that lets the other person know you look forward to seeing and talking to them again.

Skills for Interacting with Peers

When I was a principal, Ted was one of the nicest boys I knew in the sixth grade. He was just terrific at talking to grown-ups. In fact, he preferred adults to the kids in his class and hung around with the teachers on the playground. He didn't have very many friends, and I could see why. Although he had plenty of social skills that helped him get along with grown-ups, he was a total failure in the kid department.

Peers are people your own age, the kids you go to school with, and you need to have some special skills to get along with them.

Skill #1. Sharing. Sharing is very important, but you don't *always* have to share. Sometimes you'll have a good reason for not sharing, but make sure that if you don't want to share you can give your reason politely ("This belongs to my brother; it's brand-new, and my parents said I shouldn't let anyone else play with it").

When you decide that you want to share something, choose a good time and place to share, and then offer to share in a friendly and sincere way. Don't share just because you expect to get something in return.

Skill #2. Compromising. Learning how to compromise takes lots of practice. Start early in life with this lesson, and continue to practice. First you have to listen to what the other person wants to do. Then, in a calm way, tell that person what you would like to do. Last, you can offer to let the other person have his way now if you can do what you want later—or you can offer to give the other person what he wants later in exchange for getting what you want now. Take turns, in other words. Remember that sometimes you won't be able to get what you want, and you'll have to learn how to control any anger you may feel at unfairness.

Skill #3. Handling being teased. Everyone gets teased sometimes. Whether a person is tall, short, thin, fat, smart, or not smart, somebody somewhere can find a reason to tease her. When someone wears braces, glasses, or a hearing aid, she also might get teased. When someone is teasing you in an unkind way, the first thing you could try is just ignoring the teasing. There are lots of ways to do that: don't look at the person; don't talk to the person; think about other things; walk away; or you can give an "emotional shrug." An "emotional shrug" is a way of saying *I don't care* or *It doesn't matter to me* on the inside. Don't argue or disagree.

Another way to handle being teased is to stand up to the person in a quiet way. Stand up straight and face the person who is teasing you. Look him in the eye. Don't cry, turn around, or run away. Just hold your head high and give an "emotional shrug," like the one described earlier.

You could also agree with what the teaser is saying, but only if the statement is true (for example, you're wearing saddle shoes, or your parents are getting a divorce).

Skill #4. Saying no. First you have to decide whether or not you want to do what someone is asking you to do. Think about the reasons you have for saying no. Then tell the person no in a friendly way and give your reasons. Don't be afraid to stand up for what you believe. (See skill #7, handling peer pressure.)

Skill #5. Joining a group or activity that is already in progress. Joining a group or activity is a lot like joining in a conversation. First decide if you really want to join in. Then decide what you're going to say and choose a good time (during a break in the activity or before a new activity has begun). Say what you have to say in a friendly way, and make sure you pay attention to your nonverbal communication.

Skill #6. Letting people know what you think and believe, even when your peers or teachers don't feel the same way. The most important thing to remember about giving your opinion when it differs from the opinions of others in the group is to be calm and not get upset when you can't persuade others to agree with you. Then follow the steps for contributing to a discusion. If others disagree with you because you are stating a different point of view, stay calm. Don't be angry or raise your voice when you answer. Don't expect to change the way other people feel or think. The purpose of sharing your point of view is to give other people the chance to understand it.

Skill #7. Handling peer pressure. There will be lots of times when friends will ask you to do things that you don't want to do. Once you've made your decision to say no, be ready to give the reasons for your decision. Then learn to say no in lots of different ways if necessary:

- Broken record. Say several times what you have decided to do.
- Walk away from the situation.
- Give your reasons. "It's unhealthy, illegal, etc."
- Don't get involved in an argument, but don't back down.

Skill #8. Giving a compliment. Giving a compliment is saying something nice to a person about something they have done or the way they look. You may need to practice giving compliments so they sound sincere. You will be more comfortable when you have given many compliments to different people. So keep on trying.

After you have decided what you want to tell the other person, choose a good time and place. Smile when you give the compliment.

Skill #9. Accepting a compliment. If someone gives you a compliment, say, "Thank you." You can say something else if you like, but you don't have to. Be sure to speak loudly and clearly and sit or stand up straight when you're replying. Sometimes you can even return the compliment by saying something like, "It was very thoughtful of you to notice."

Some people get embarrassed when they are given a compliment. Others actually argue with the person giving the compliment as if trying to talk them out of it. Others act as if they don't believe what the person is saying. Don't do any of those things.

Skill #10. Apologizing. Decide if you need to tell someone that you are sorry for something you did. Think about whether you should do it in person or in writing. Apologize where you can be alone with the person, and be sincere.

Skill #11. Playing a group game or taking part in a group activity. If you're going to play a group game, be sure you know the rules. Don't forget to wait your turn. When the game is over, say something nice to someone else who was also playing the game.

Skill #12. Handling being left out or verbally rejected. When somebody isn't nice to you, try using the emotional shrug. Sometimes that works when you're not too upset. When you're really feeling left out, do something nice for yourself like lying down in a comfortable place, reading a favorite book, playing your favorite tape or CD, or going for a walk with your dog. Tell yourself, *It's okay to make mistakes. It's only human. This could happen to anyone. I'm sorry I messed up, but it isn't the end of the world. Sure, I made a mistake, but I've done so many other things so well.*

Skill #13. Handling someone asking you to do something you can't do because you don't know how. If someone asks you to do something you can't do because you don't know how (like swimming, bowling, or roller skating), be honest from the very beginning. If you pretend you can do something you can't, you'll only be embarrassed in the end. Say, "I'm sorry, but I never learned how to play volleyball (or swim)." Ask, "Can I just watch this time? Maybe I'll try it later." Or, "If you explain the rules to me, I'll try my best."

Skill #14. Suggesting an activity to the group. If you want to suggest an activity to the group, decide what you will say ahead of time. Choose a good time to make your suggestion. Don't interrupt, and say it in a friendly way.

Skill #15. Seeking help (or a favor) from peers. Sometimes you'll need to ask for help from a friend.

Once you've decided that you can't do something alone, plan what you want to say. Then ask for help in a pleasant way (raising your hand or going up to the person). Be ready to wait if they can't help you or give you the favor right away, and remember to say thank you to the person.

Skill #16. Asking a question. Remember to first ask yourself if you already know the answer. Don't ask questions just to get attention. After you decide what you need to ask and who you will ask, then decide how you will ask. Make sure you choose a good time and place to get the person's attention. Then ask your question, and thank the person for giving you the answer.

Skill #17. Saying thank you. You can never go wrong saying thank you. Once you've decided you want to thank someone, think about the best way to say it.

- Say, "Thank you for . . ."
- Say, "I really like the present you gave me."
- Remember to do something nice for that person sometime later.

Skill #18. Keeping a secret. If you don't think you can keep the secret, ask your friend not to tell you. When someone tells you a secret, try to forget about it, and don't talk about it to anyone else.

Skill #19. Disagreeing. First listen to the other person's side of the argument. Then tell your side of the argument. See if you can find something you both agree on.

Be fair and friendly, and if you can't agree, don't continue to argue. If necessary, ask an adult to help you.

Skills for Controlling Emotions

I could hear his tantrums well before he and his teacher reached the office. His name was Larry, and he was in the second grade. He was a smart little boy, but he had absolutely no emotional control.

When Larry wasn't chosen first in gym, he lost his temper. When somebody else got to the drinking fountain first, Larry threw a punch at the person. Even during recess, a time that was supposed to be relaxing and fun, Larry was usually upset. He got mad when he couldn't kick the ball, and even madder when somebody on his team misplaced a kick. Larry was a pretty miserable little person, and so were all of the people who had to spend time with him.

Most of all, I felt sorry for his mom. Larry really had a hard time with self-control at home. If you share a few of Larry's bad habits, you can learn a new set of social skills that will help you control your feelings.

Skill #1. Identifying and expressing your emotions. See if you can figure out how you feel, and decide what you should call the feeling. Here are some common ways we all feel from time to time: nervous, anxious, disappointed, depressed, annoyed, angry, furious, hateful, jealous, envious, upset, happy, joyful, sad, elated, excited, uptight, tense, jittery, jumpy, confused, uncertain, frightened, or fearful. When you figure out how you are feeling, it's OK to say to yourself or to others, "I feel . . ."

Skill #2. Handling other people's anger. When other people get angry at you, first listen to what they are saying. Then make a choice to:

- Keep listening.
- Ask the person why he is angry.
- Give him an idea about how to fix the problem.
- Walk away for now.

Skill #3. Handling your own anger. First stop and count to ten or breathe deeply. Then think about your choices. You can calmly tell the person why you are angry, or you can walk away for now.

Skill #4. Handling another person's failure or mistakes. Try to think of how you feel when you make a mistake and how you want to be treated. Then treat that person the way you would like to be treated if you were her. Don't laugh or tease. If the person seems embarrassed, just go on with what you are doing. Sometime later you could talk to her privately, tell her you know how she feels, and encourage her.

Skill #5. Handling your own failure. Decide if you have failed, and then think about why you failed. Think about what you could do differently next time. Think about a positive self-statement you might make to yourself, like:

- I think I can do it.
- I can give this a good try.
- I can be a responsible person.
- I'm still OK even if I make a mistake.
- If I try, I can do it.
- I can control myself if I work at it.
- Even if I fail, I can always try again.
- I can make things happen if I work at it.
- If I keep on working, I'll improve.
- I can improve each time I try.

Then make a plan about what to do next time.

Skill #6. Handling losing. Say to yourself, *Somebody has to lose. It's OK that I didn't win,* and then think about your choices:

- Talk to someone you trust about how you feel.
- Do an activity you like to do.
- Do a relaxation exercise, like breathing deeply.
- Think of what you can honestly tell the person who won. ("Congratulations, you played a good game. You're getting a lot better at this game.")

Skill #7. Expressing affection. Decide if you have good feelings about the other person, and then decide if you think the other person would like to know that you feel this way. Decide what you will say, and choose a good time and place. Tell the person in a friendly way.

Skill #8. Dealing with fear. Decide if you are feeling afraid and what you are afraid of. Then think about your choices:

- Talk to someone about it.
- Do a relaxation exercise.
- Do something else to take your mind off your fear.
- Confront your fear if it is something you are afraid of doing, and try it anyway if it is something good to do.

Skill #9. Rewarding yourself. Decide if you did a good job, and say to yourself, *I did a good job.* Decide how else you could reward yourself (maybe with a treat, a short break, or a telephone conversation with a friend).

Skill #10. Using self-control. Stop and count to ten. Then think about how your body feels. Think about your choices:

- Walk away for now.
- Do a relaxation exercise.
- Write about how you feel.
- Talk to someone about it.

Skill #11. Handling embarrassment. Decide what happened to cause you to feel embarrassed and think of what you can do to feel less embarrassed. You might ignore it, decide what to do next time, or say to yourself, *It's over. People will forget it.*

Skill #12. Accepting no. Decide why you were told no, and then think about your choices:

- Do something else.

- Say how you feel, in a friendly way.
- Write about how you feel.

I hope that reading this chapter has helped you to think in a new way about the important things you can begin to do today to make and keep friends. The process won't always be easy, especially if you've gone for a long time without friends, but you'll be surprised at the results if you just try.

5

Fifty Fabulous Activities to Build Friendship Skills at Home

Sponge activities" is a term we in education use to describe short learning activities that "sponge" up time that might otherwise be wasted. They maximize learning! Following are some "sponge-like activities" to help you and your family build and sustain a cooperative and friendly family environment. If you use these activities, not only will your family life improve, but your child will begin to develop a repertoire of healthy social skills.

1. Put Yourself in the Picture
Be on the lookout for interesting scenarios or situations as you travel, read newspapers, look at pic-

tures, or overhear conversations. Point them out to your child. After both you and your child have observed what is going on, ask the question: "How would *you* feel (physically, emotionally) if this were happening to you?" Observations can be retold at the dinner table if only one person observes the scenario. This exercise helps to build empathy and understanding for others and encourages our children to "walk in another's shoes," a skill they will need if they are to make and keep friends.

2. Secret Buddies (Secret Santa, Secret Pal)

This activity goes by many names, but the principle is always the same—each family member anonymously buys inexpensive gifts or does small acts of kindness for another family member over a short period of time. Our family always did this the week before Christmas and left small gifts in special places. When the children were too young to go to town by themselves, I dropped them off in a shopping area and had a cup of coffee while I waited for them to return. We derived more enjoyment from this activity than from opening our presents on Christmas morning. Write the name of each family member on a small piece of paper and place these in a hat (or other container). Draw names and set the guidelines for what family members should be doing for their buddies (gifts, favors, notes, cards). At the end of the specified time period, everyone tries to guess who their Secret Buddy is.

3. Jigsaw Puzzles

Putting together jigsaw puzzles as a family project can foster cooperation and teamwork. Spread the pieces out on a large table where they can be left undisturbed for a period of time. "Neat freaks" need not sign on for this activity. Determine the guidelines, if any (e.g., the edge has to be finished before you can start the inside). The age of your children will determine the complexity of the puzzle you choose. Our recent puzzle when the children were home for a visit (ages 23 and 25) was a 1000-piece photo of a complete set of major league baseball caps. There is always a sense of shared accomplishment when a puzzle has been completed. We take a picture of the completed puzzle, before it is dismantled, as a record of our work.

4. Small Talk

Small talk is an important social convention—the ability to chat about inconsequential and relatively unimportant topics as conversational transitions. The weather, sports, travel, family happenings, etc. are all subjects for small talk. Small talk bridges the gap between awkward silence and moving on to more meaningful conversation. Small talk takes place when you encounter people in shopping malls, run into them after church, or see them at the health club.

Practice small talk at the dinner table, pretending that family members are relatively new acquaintances who are trying to decide whether they want to get to know each other better.

5. Family Traditions

Dolores Curran, in her book *Traits of a Healthy Family*, suggests that every family take time to list their traditions—the dozens, even hundreds of little rituals that are unique to their family. Here's part of a list of traditions drawn up by one family at a seminar in which each family was given five minutes to think of and write down their family traditions and rituals.

- Youngest child always blows out the candles.
- Wednesday is leftover night.
- Waffles every Sunday morning.
- Taking-down-the-tree party every January 1.
- We leave notes on the refrigerator.

Take some time to make a list of your family traditions. Begin to make some new ones, too. Investigate books like *Family Celebrations at Thanksgiving, Family Celebrations at Christmas,* and *Family Celebrations at Easter* by Ann Hibbard (Baker).

6. Bedtime Chats

One-on-one time with your child is extremely important. Take a few minutes each evening to say goodnight and have a bedtime chat. Debrief the day, read a bedtime story, or share a funny anecdote. Begin this practice when your child is small, and chances are you won't have problems communicating when he reaches the teen years.

7. Christmas or Thanksgiving Sharing

Establish a family tradition of sharing with a family in need of financial assistance during the holiday season. Your church or neighborhood social agencies can usually put you in touch with someone. Purchase everything they will need to have a complete Thanksgiving or Christmas.

8. Miss a Meal for a Purpose

If your children are old enough to understand and manage the concept of fasting, plan to miss a meal together and give the cost of that meal to the missions fund or a local food bank.

9. Shine Where You Are

Practice politeness at home. Use "Please," "Thank you," and "Excuse me" regularly with other family members. Don't yell or raise your voice. Avoid criticizing one another or making critical remarks about yourself. Try it for a week, and then assess your progress in a family meeting.

10. Shine in Your Neighborhood

Choose a family or individual in your neighborhood for whom you will do a good deed. Bake some cookies, take their garbage cans out to the curb, shovel their walk, bring them a bouquet of flowers, or leave a cheery note or card in their mailbox.

11. Make a Friend

Concentrate for a period of time (week, month) on making new acquaintances and friends. Keep track of each family member's "new friends" on a chart. To qualify for the chart, the family member must know the new acquaintance's name and be able to tell one important fact about the person.

12. C.A.P.

Read aloud the story *Cap It Off with a Smile* by Robin Inwald (New York: Hilson Press, 1994). Practice the "cap it off" strategy, which includes: 1) giving Compliments to our friends and people we know; 2) **A**sking questions to show that we have an interest in what our friends are doing; and 3) always being **P**ositive in our outlook. Cap off whatever you do with a smile. This simple acronym highlights some very basic social skills.

13. Turkey Trot

If you have younger children in your family, you can literally cut out turkeys from brown construction paper, one for each family member. Write each individual's name on the turkey. Pass the turkeys around the table. Write a compliment or something to be thankful for about each family member.

14. Charades

One person (or team) decides upon a slogan, proverb, or title of a book, poem, song, TV show, or movie. She then acts it out, and the other person or team must guess the answer. Individual words can also be pantomimed. The purpose of this game is to help children who are unable to perceive (and express) nonverbal cues of attitudes, intentions, and moods practice these skills.

15. Silent Cheer

As the family sits around the dinner table, have each family member talk about something he did particularly well that day. After each recitation, the rest of the family members will give a silent cheer.

16. Kudos

As the family sits around the dinner table, have each family member give the family member to the

right a compliment. Comments need to be detailed
and descriptive of something meaningful that a family
member has been or done. No glowing generalities!
Be specific.

17. Feelings

As the family sits around the dinner table, have
each family member describe a feeling she had during
the day and the circumstances surrounding that feeling. In preparation for this activity, take some time
to discuss a variety of feelings (e.g., nervous, anxious,
disappointed, depressed, annoyed, angry, furious,
hateful, jealous, envious, upset, happy, joyful, sad,
elated, excited, uptight, tense, jittery, jumpy, confused,
uncertain, frightened, fearful).

18. The Question

The chairperson (this assignment can rotate from
meal to meal) asks each family member "The Question."
The question can vary, but here are some examples:

- Tell me something you like about yourself.
- Tell me something you felt good about today.
- Tell me something you're happy about.
- Tell me something you're learning to do
  better.

19. It Isn't Easy Being Green

Each family member identifies something about
himself that's a bit of a challenge to handle.

- It's not easy being the youngest. (Explain
  why.)

- It's not easy working all day and then coming home and having to fix dinner.
- It's not easy being clumsy.

20. Jigsaw

This jigsaw is different from the puzzle we were working on earlier. This is a cooperative learning technique in which a learning task is divided up among the members of the group. Each member "learns" his material and then teaches it to the other members of the group. This activity works best with older children. This activity could be used if you are planning a vacation and want to learn about the place you are going. Each family member could read something about the place and then tell the family what she has learned.

21. Abraham's Walk of Faith

This activity is taken from *Family Celebration at Thanksgiving* by Ann Hibbard (Baker Books, 1995) and is a good trust-builder. Divide your family into pairs. In each pair, one will be the follower and the other will be the leader. The follower puts on a blindfold and cannot see anything. First have the leader spin the follower around so that the follower is disoriented. Then the leader must lead the follower around the yard or house, using only verbal directions. The older the players, the more complex and circuitous a route they can take. When the leader has returned to the starting point with the follower, the follower should take off the blindfold. Pay special attention to safety considerations when playing this game. Leaders need to be completely trustworthy.

22. Heroes of the Faith Charade

Each player is given a turn to be the actor. The actor selects a hero of faith from the Bible (for example, David, Jonah, Moses, Samuel, Joseph) and has three minutes to convey (without words) the identity of this character. The actor can do this by pantomiming scenes from this character's life. Other players, of course, must try to guess the character. The person with the right answer takes the next turn unless he has already had a turn, in which case that person may give the turn to someone who has not yet been the actor. (Taken from *Family Celebration at Thanksgiving* by Ann Hibbard (Baker Books, 1995).

23. Wanted for Being . . .

Each family member makes a wanted poster similar to those found in the Old West. Use poster board or large pieces of white construction paper. In addition to the usual portrait of the individual who is wanted, this poster will have a list of positive qualities under the picture that describe the individual. For example, "Wanted for being . . ."

- a good cook
- a thoughtful person
- the mother of Ryan and Julie
- the best Checkers player in the state

24. Turn Off the TV and Turn On to Reading (and other things also)

There is well-documented research regarding the detrimental effects of television viewing and that should convince you, even if I can't, that turning off your TV will be beneficial for your children. Dr. Thomas Lickona, in his wonderful book *Raising Good Children,* suggests trying some of the following activities in lieu of the "terrible tube."

- Read (a book, a magazine, the paper), together or alone.
- Play (inside or out).
- Exercise (take a walk, ride your bike, jog, play a sport).
- Help with the housework or yardwork.
- Have a friend over, or visit a friend.
- Do a good deed for a neighbor.
- Do your homework.
- Practice a musical instrument.
- Listen to the radio, records, tapes, or CDs. (Tapes of old radio shows are great for stimulating imagination.)
- Finish an unfinished project.
- Play a board game.
- Work on a hobby.
- Cook something special together.
- Go to a movie, play, concert, or museum.
- Go on a hike or picnic.
- Go somewhere you've never been before.
- Visit someone who's sick or shut in.
- Write a letter to someone who'd like to hear from you.

25. The Committee

This is a popular activity for us and many of our twelve grandchildren. When we arrive for a week-long visit to care for the children while their parents vacation, we immediately form a committee. Someone is designated the chairperson, someone is selected secretary, and the meeting is called to order. Each member of the committee (including Grandma and Grandpa) takes his or her turn in making a suggestion for an after-school activity (e.g., bowling, shopping at Wal-Mart, watching a video, going out to eat at Fuddruckers, etc.). Once the list is complete, the group decides if any of the activities are too expensive or too impractical (e.g., going to Disneyland, buying new dirt bikes). The suggestions that are approved by the group are each written on a small piece of paper. These are placed in a hat. Each afternoon after school, a new suggestion is drawn and implemented. There are no arguments, and everyone agrees. The committee could be used to generate suggestions for meals, things to do during an at-home vacation, or anything else you need consensus about.

26. Make a Family Poster

This is a great activity for a rainy vacation day. You will need markers, construction paper, glue, family photos, magazines, and lots of creativity. Create a poster that represents your family. It should include pictures of family members, things you like to do together, places you have gone, and interesting facts about everyone. Hang the poster on your refrigerator for everyone to enjoy.

27. Role Reversal

Rather than telling your kids how they make you feel, ask these questions to create some role reversal in your family. "How do you think I feel when I work hard to fix a nice dinner, and you don't come when you're called?" "What would you do if you found out that your child had lied to you?" "What kind of advice would you give to parents who were having a hard time getting their kids to do chores?" (From an idea suggested by Dr. Thomas Lickona in *Raising Good Children,* New York: Bantam Books, 1983.)

28. Conversations Kids Crave

Torey Hayden, in an article in *Families* magazine entitled "Conversations Kids Crave," reported the results of a study in which several hundred children and teenagers were asked what they really wished their parents would talk to them about. Eight topics were mentioned most frequently.

- *Family matters.* Kids want to be informed about what is going on in their family: jobs, money problems, death, illness, divorce. . . . They usually know if something serious is happening, and not letting them in on the real story creates even more anxiety. They also want to have some input into decisions that involve them (vacations, allowances, bedtime).
- *Controversial issues.* Sex, drugs, morals, and values rank high on the list of topics kids wish parents wouldn't just avoid because they are uncomfortable or embarassed.
- *Emotional issues.* Kids want their parents to say those three little words. And those words are not "No, you can't!"
- *The big whys.* Kids want to know about God, the meaning of life, war, hunger, and death.

74

You don't have to know all the answers, but kids need to know that as well.

- *The future.* Kids, especially those who are approaching adolescence, want to talk about what the future holds—college, career, marriage, etc.
- *Current events.* The news is a constant source of anxiety and wonder for children. Talk about the things that happen (random violence, war, hunger).
- *Personal interests.* Show an interest in the friends, hobbies, and extracurricular activities of your child.
- *Parents themselves.* Kids love to hear stories of how things used to be. Don't pay any attention to those groans you hear—they love to hear you talk.

29. Hold a Conversation

Do you find yourself at a loss for words when seated across from your six-year-old at McDonald's? Keep these conversation starters suggested by Dr. Thomas Lickona in your back pocket, and pull one out when silence falls.

- How was today on a scale of 1 to 10 (where 1 is terrible and 10 is terrific)? What made it that way?
- What was the high point (or low point) of your day?
- Tell me the good news and the bad news about school today (work today, practice this week, camp this summer)?

- What's a thought or feeling you had today?
- What happened today that you didn't expect?
- (If your child seems preoccupied) I'm wondering what you're thinking about. Would you be willing to talk to me about it?

If you haven't seen your child for a period of time, try these conversation starters:

- Tell me about something good that's happened since the last time we talked.
- What's something you've done recently that you're proud of?
- What's on your mind these days?
- What are you looking forward to these days?

30. Organizing the Family Photos
Enlist the help of everyone to organize the family photos. There will be many positive outcomes from this activity: a chance to relive happy memories, a chance to teach kids how to break an unmanageable task into small chunks and finish it; and a well-organized and accessible photo collection.

31. This House Is a Mess
When you think you can't stand it anymore, gather the family together for a council meeting. Talk about how everyone could pitch in to get the house cleaned up in a short time. "Many hands make light work," as my mother always used to say. On a large sheet of paper, list all of the jobs that need to be done, then assign different family members to each task, depending on

age, skill level, and interest. Post the list in a prominent place in the house so that as individual members complete their task (and have it inspected by the foreman—usually Mom), they can cross it off. Order in pizza or take the gang out to McDonald's for lunch. No one will want to dirty the clean house!

32. Thinking Ahead

Children need opportunities to think through how they might handle emergencies. Brainstorm a list of possible problems that could occur to your children (consider their ages when putting the list together), and then choose a problem for discussion and problem solving (e.g., a flat tire on the expressway, getting locked out when no one's home, or rescuing a bird that has flown down the fireplace chimney and is flying around the house—an incident that actually happened at our house while I was at work).

33. Going the Extra Mile

As a family, be on the lookout for people you meet who go the extra mile. You will need to explain this concept to your children and give them examples (e.g., the secretary who helps them find their lost backpack, the store clerk who searches in the back room for the toy you can't find on the shelf, the carry-out person at the grocery store who cheerfully bundles everything into your car, the mail person who puts the package in a plastic bag when it's raining, etc.). Post the names of these people on your refrigerator, and write thank-you notes to them from your family. This exercise will sensitize your child to the importance of service.

34. The No Nagging Week

Every family has people and problems that result in nagging—like a child who doesn't make his bed, or a spouse who doesn't throw dirty clothes in the hamper. These problems often result in verbal nagging that rarely does any good. As a family, vow to suspend all nagging for one week and to write Post-It messages instead.

35. Now and Then

An enlightening after-dinner conversation can revolve around what things were like "when I was a kid." Compare automobiles, prices, restaurants, movies, television programs, spare-time activities, etc.

36. Information Hunt

Teach your children how to do research when they need information about something. If you're going to buy something, let kids search out ads; if you're looking for shops that can repair your broken clock, let the kids find them in the yellow pages; if you're doing a crossword puzzle, let the kids look up the meanings you can't figure out. Emphasize the idea that you can always find the answer in a resource somewhere. Go to the public library and consult with the reference librarian if you can't find your answer anywhere else.

37. Rate Your Involvement IQ

Periodically take stock of your meaningful involvement in your child's life. How often do you eat meals with your child? read aloud? have a conversation about her day? When was the last time you listened to your child explain her point of view that was different from yours? Have you worked on any joint projects with your child lately? Have you been involved in any way in your child's school? How many school events (sports, concerts) have you attended? If you can't answer positively to all of these, take some time to schedule your child back into your life.

38. Who Needs My Help?

This exercise as well as the next three are taken from the book *Bringing Up a Moral Child* by Michael Schulman and Evan Mekler (New York: Doubleday, 1984). Target an individual with whom your child interacts on a regular basis (perhaps a sibling, friend, grandparent, or parent). Develop a chart that includes the heading: *When* does he/she need help? *Why* does he/she need help? *What* help does he/she need? *How* can I help? *When* I helped.

39. What Did I Do?

This exercise or game will help your child think about his actions and their impact on the people close to him. For each day that you will be engaging in this exercise, give your child a chart that contains the following questions: What did I do today that made _____ feel good? Why? What did I do today that made _____ feel bad? Why? The blank can be filled in with the name of anyone you want to encourage your child to think about more sensitively.

40. What Will I Do?

This exercise is similar to the previous one, with the exception that questions are changed to What will

I do to make _____ feel good (or bad)? and
Why?

41. Sherlock Holmes Game

This game helps your children (especially younger
elementary age) to be sensitive to the likes and dis-
likes of people they know. They will be detectives, like
Sherlock Holmes, carefully observing everything that
is being said and done. Make a chart with the following questions:

The CASE: _____
(name of the person being observed):

	When?	Why?	How Do You Know?
Likes			
Dislikes			

After making these observations, the final step in
the game is making the leap from observation to ac-
tion—determining what the child can do to make the
person feel good.

42. Family Council/Family Meetings

Many families have regularly scheduled family
meetings once a week or twice a month. Issues and
problems are discussed, and brainstorming takes
place about how problems could be solved. Some families have a special meal together; others go out to
dinner after the family meeting. To have successful
meetings, all members need to participate, and re-
spect for everyone's opinion must be maintained.

43. Are You Convincing?

Ernest, Rita, and Paul Siegel, in their book *Help for the Lonely Child,* suggest a game in which a child steps into the shoes of another and role-plays a "convincing argument." Some of the situations that might be enacted:

- Convince a clerk to let you return something that is unreturnable.
- Convince your parents that you need a new bike.
- Convince the teacher that homework should be abolished.
- Convince someone to give up a bad habit, like smoking.

44. Board and Card Games

Board and card games are wonderful tools for practicing social skills. Set aside a regular time each week, review the rules of sportsmanship and behavior, and set the timer so that there will be no arguments about bedtime.

45. Role-Playing

This is a wonderful technique for learning and practicing new social skills. Even teenagers can benefit from role-playing from time to time (e.g., going in to see the teacher because of a failing grade; telling the coach you're going to drop out of football).

46. Family Devotions

These will never happen without a plan and commitment, but they are a critical and meaningful part of building family friendships. If you have memories of interminable prayers and incomprehensible passages of Scripture from your childhood, do some browsing at your Christian bookstore to find ideas for child-proofing your family devotions.

47. Family Goal-Setting
Consider your family to be an organization just like the business for which you work. Every organization has yearly goals, which are evaluated at the end of the year before new ones are set. Why not set two or three goals for your family this year, develop a plan and timeline to carry out these goals, and then get busy? You'll be amazed at what you can accomplish if you actually gather the family together and brainstorm.

48. Real Work
I started working for my father in his grocery store when I was six years old—stocking baby food on empty shelves and putting potatoes in paper sacks. It was real work, and even then I was proud to be helping my dad. Nowadays kids don't have many opportunities to do real jobs. Make sure that your children have a chance to do something real, either around your house or at the office.

49. Open Up Your Home
Plan social events with another compatible family. Learning to get along and appreciate the unique personalities and lifestyles of other families will enrich yours.

50. Problems, Problems, Problems

Healthy families are realistic about their problems. They talk about them and work at solving them. Develop your own unique problem-solving method, give it a name (e.g., the Sticky Situation Solver), and use it routinely when problems arise in your family. It's far more beneficial to recognize and face problems head-on than to sweep them under the rug.

Friendship begins at home. Your child's first and best friend can and should be you, her parent. Begin now to create a friendly atmosphere in your home where your child can learn and practice how to be a friend. Enjoy your child. Affirm his uniqueness and support him when he needs help. If you hear the refrain "Nobody likes me" at your house, respond this way: "I like you, and I'll help you learn how to make friends."

Resources for Parents

Briggs, Dorothy Corkille. *Your Child's Self Esteem: The Key to His Life.* New York: Doubleday, 1970.

Cartledge, Gwendolyn, and JoAnne Fellows Milburn. *Teaching Social Skills to Children and Youth.* New York: Allyn and Bacon, 1995.

Eyre, Richard, and Linda Eyre. *Teaching Your Children Values.* New York: Simon & Schuster, 1993.

Goldstein, Arnold P.; Robert P. Sprafkin; N. Jane Gershaw; and Paul Klein. *Skillstreaming the Adolescent: A Structured Learning Approach to Teaching Prosocial Skills.* Champaign, Ill.: Research Press, 1980.

Goldstein, Sam, and Michael Goldstein. *Managing Attention Disorders in Children.* New York: John Wiley and Sons, 1990.

Lickona, Thomas. *Raising Good Children.* New York: Bantam Books, 1983.

McGinnis, Ellen, and Arnold P. Goldstein. *Skillstreaming the Elementary School Child.* Champaign, Ill.: Research Press, 1984.

Phillips, Deborah. *How to Give Your Child a Great Self-Image.* New York: Random House, 1989.

Reuben, Steven Carr. *Raising Ethical Children.* Rocklin, Calif.: Prima Publishing, 1994.

Rubin, Zick. *Children's Friendships.* Cambridge, Mass.: Harvard University Press, 1980.

Schulman, Michael and Eva Mekler. *Bringing Up a Moral Child.* New York: Doubleday, 1994.

Siegel, Ernest; Rita Siegel; and Paul Siegel. *Help for the Lonely Child: Strengthening Social Perception.* New York: E.P. Dutton, 1974.